This book belongs to

_____

Humble Ninja

By Mary Nhin

Pictures by
Jelena Stupar

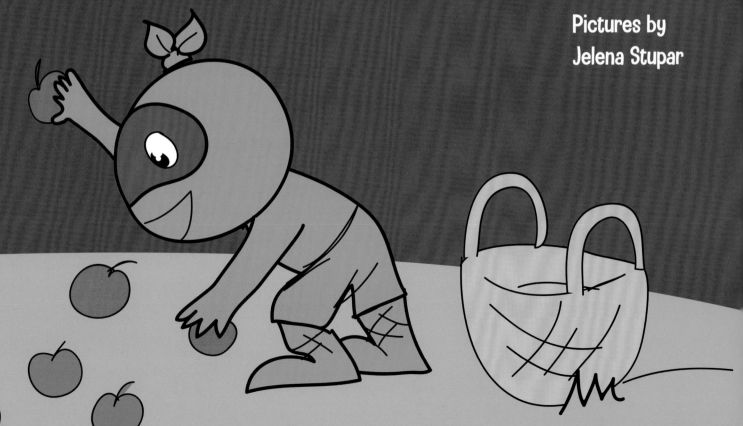

I don't think less of myself. I just think of myself less.

For example...

When I'm working on something, I ask for a second opinion.

If I do something wrong, I acknowledge my mistake and apologize.

When someone does something nice, I say thank you. It makes me feel happy inside and lifts me up like a balloon.

There was a time, though, when I didn't show as much humility...

Everyone had gotten their spelling tests
back and I was showing off my grade.

At the time, I didn't understand that bragging could hurt other people's feelings.

Later that day, Visionary Ninja was showing everyone a **Humble Pie**.

In a Humble Pie, there are 4 ingredients that start with the letter 'A':

Avoid bragging

Appreciate others

Apologize when you are wrong

Ask for feedback

Avoid bragging

Bragging is when you talk about how the things that you do or own are better than someone else. Sometimes, it makes people feel bad because they don't have it or can't do it, and then they become sad.

How would you feel if the roles were reversed and you didn't get picked for the team and your friend did?

Everyone wants to brag, sometimes. We want to share our accomplishments. It's okay to tell family or close friends, because they understand and they are excited. It isn't okay to say it in front of a friend that doesn't have it or can't do it. We can make them feel bad.

Appreciate others

Saying thank you right away when someone does something nice
is a great way to show your appreciation. When we are grateful,
we are happy.

Apologize when you are wrong

When we make mistakes, it's great to admit to them.

Ask for feedback

As we go through life, no matter how old we get or how much we've learned, we always have something more to learn. A humble person recognizes that no matter how much he thinks he knows, he can still improve.

The next day at school everyone got their progress reports.

I could tell some of my classmates weren't too happy about their reports, so I decided not to share. I didn't want any of my classmates to feel sad because I got good grades, and they didn't.

Later that day, I celebrated with my mother and father. I felt happy about working hard to get those grades! And I was even happier I learned something new about being humble.

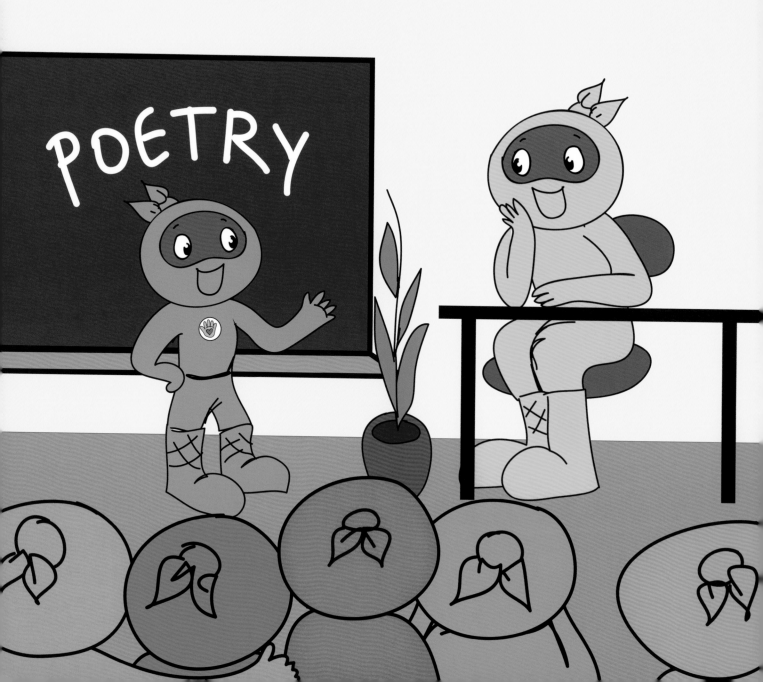

I don't always know the answers.
And I recognize that I'm not always right.
There are things I can learn.
I will always keep that in sight.

I don't want others to feel lonely or sad.
So I'll think twice before speaking my words.
It's important to me that they are included
Because I want others to be heard.

When I am wrong,
I'll say sorry right away.
Because there's no point
In arguing and fighting all day.

I am blessed with people in my life
Who support and help me.
I look forward to saying thank you
Because being grateful keeps me happy.

Eating more Humble Pie could be your secret weapon against arrogance and conceit.

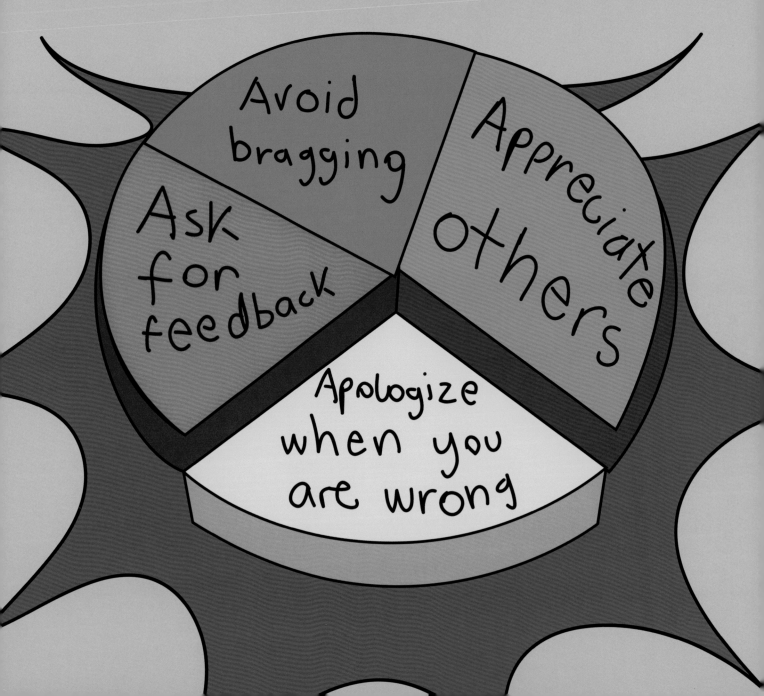

Please visit us at ninjalifehacks.tv for fun, free printables.

@marynhin   @GrowGrit
#NinjaLifeHacks

Mary Nhin   Ninja Life Hacks

Ninja Life Hacks